Merry

CHRISTMAS

This Books Belongs To

....

....

....

....

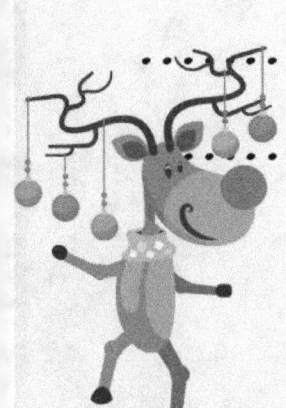

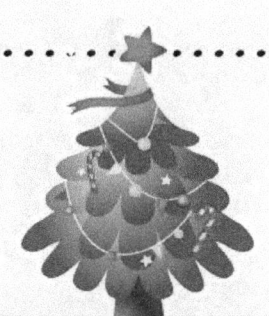

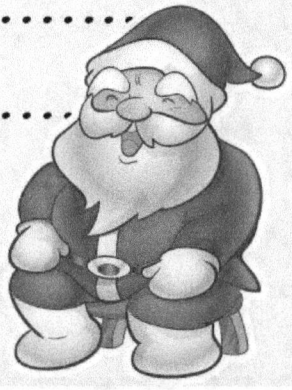

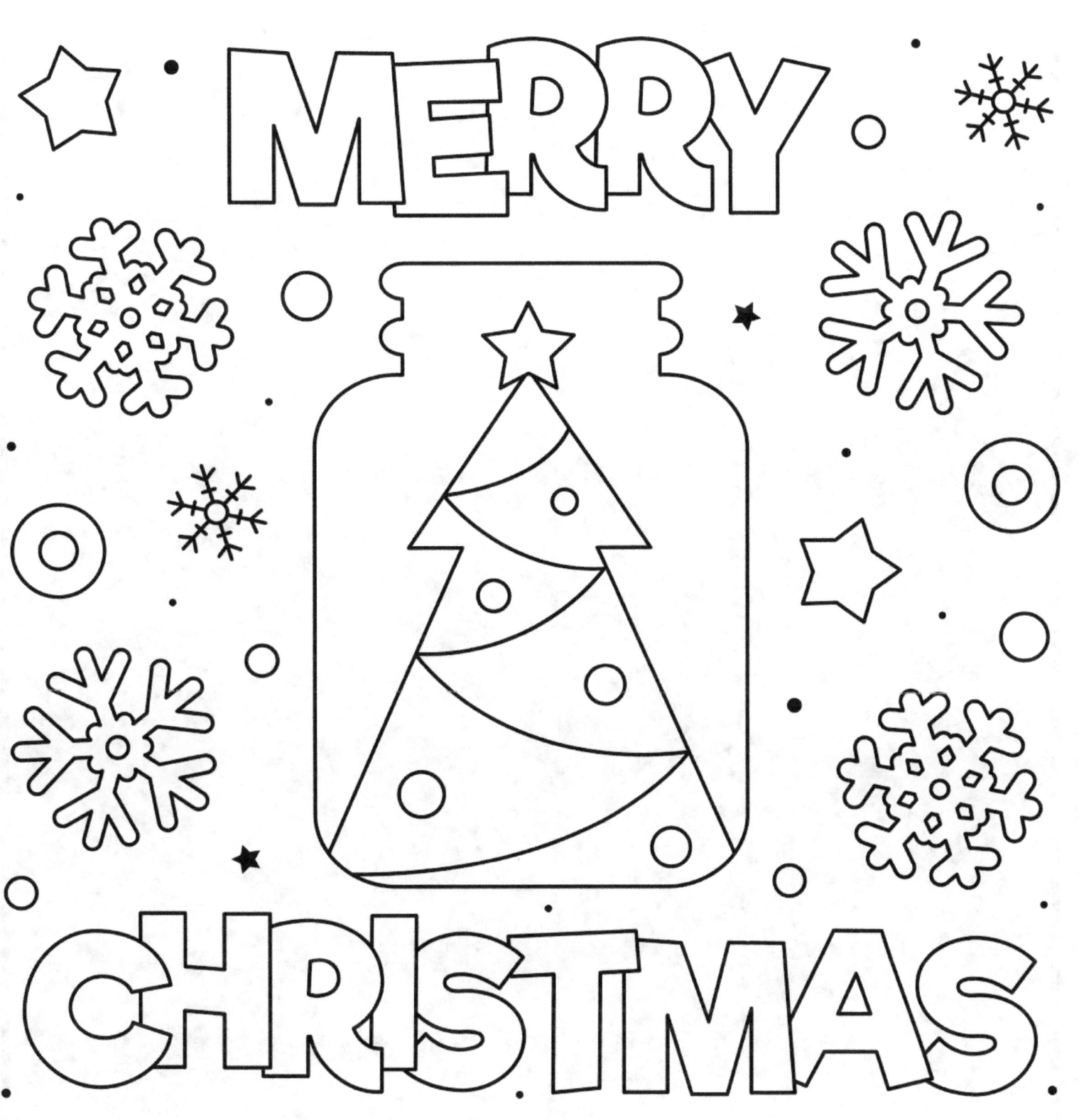

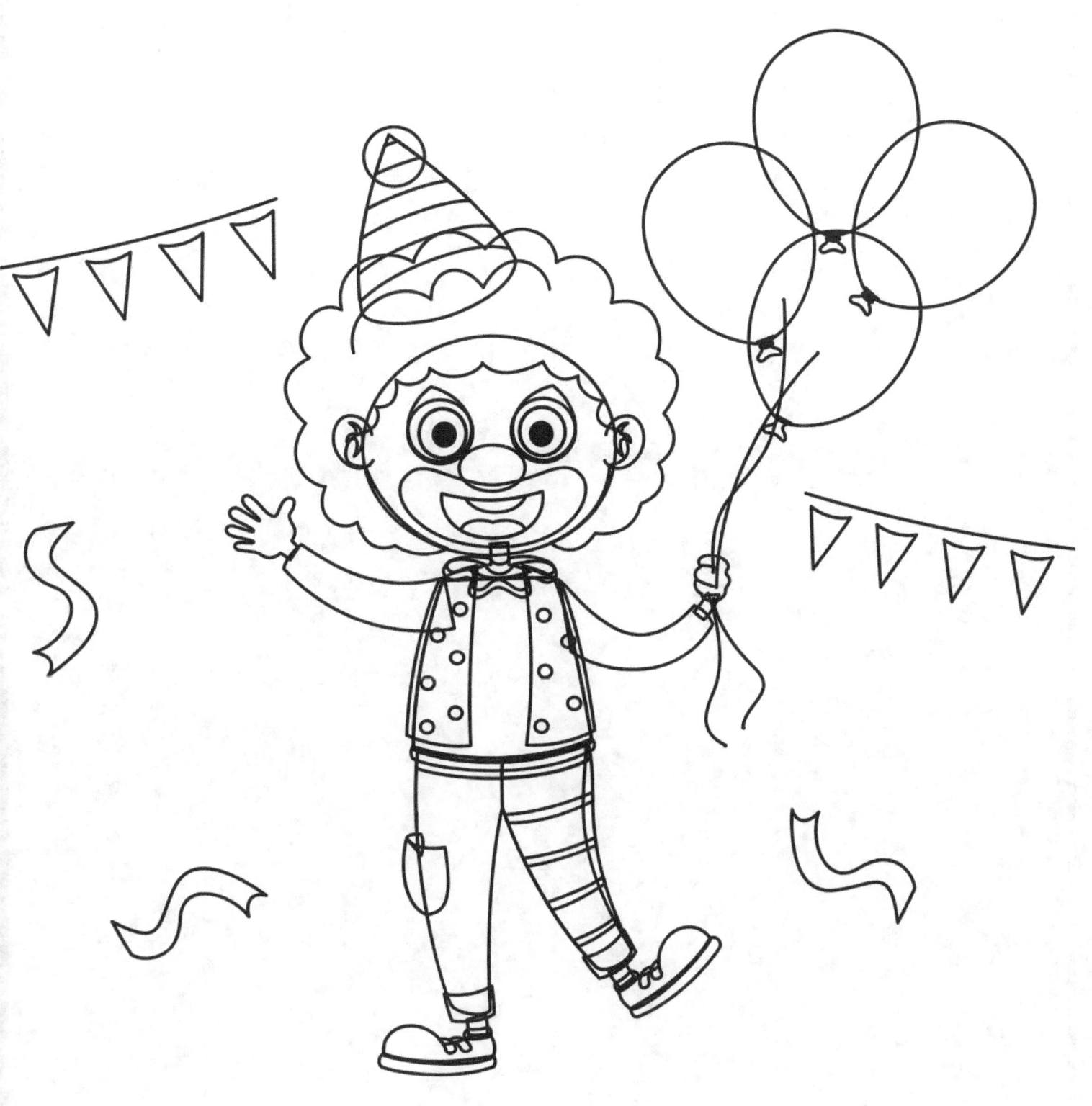

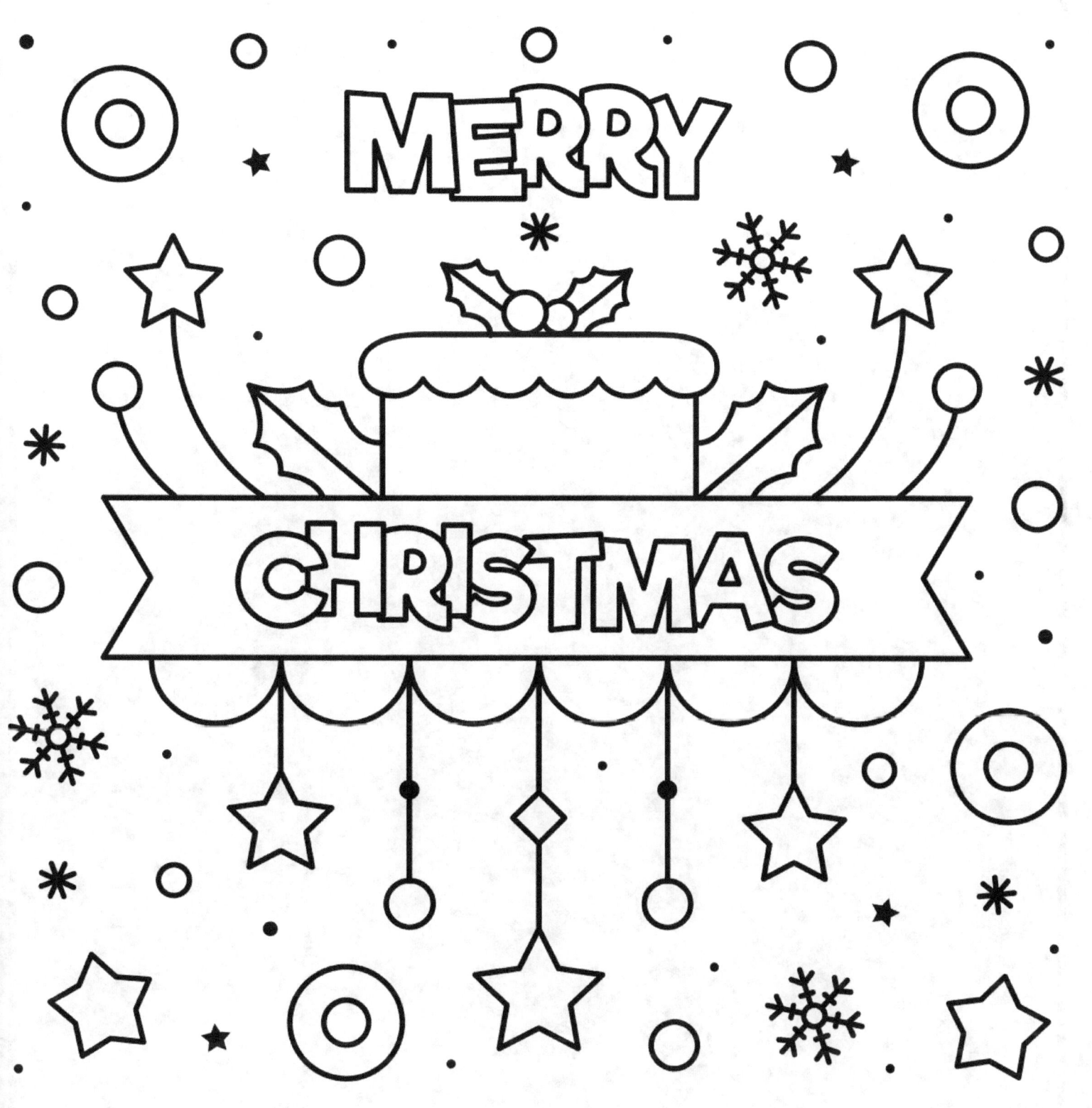

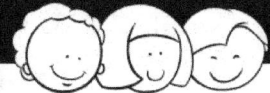

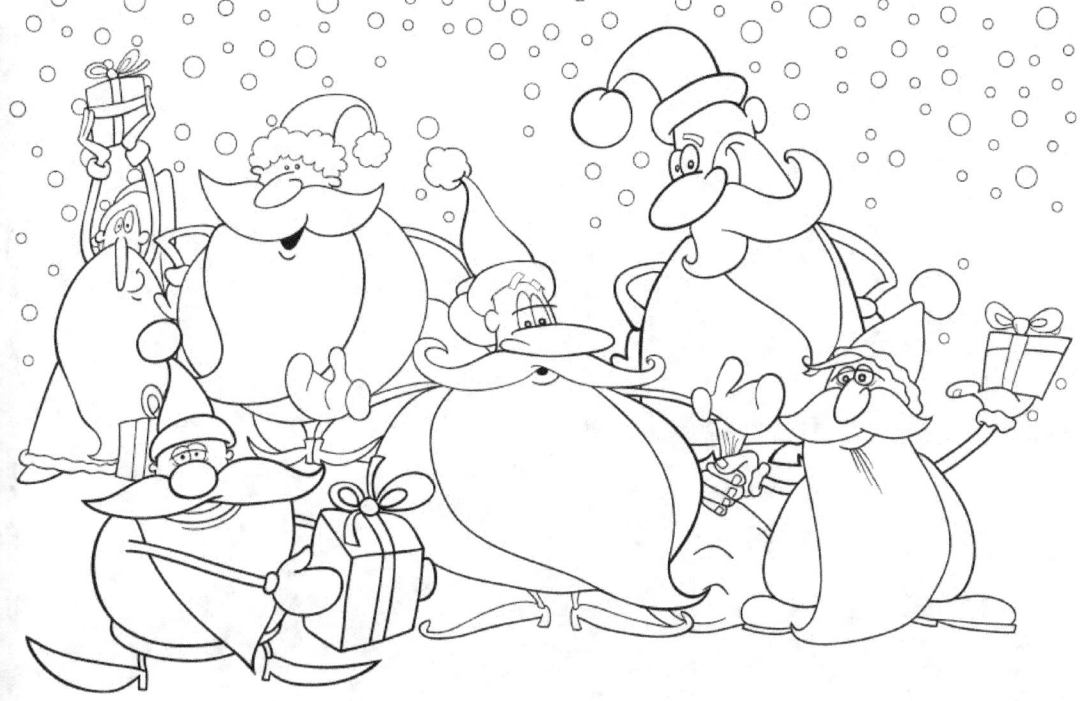

FIND

7

DIFFERENCES

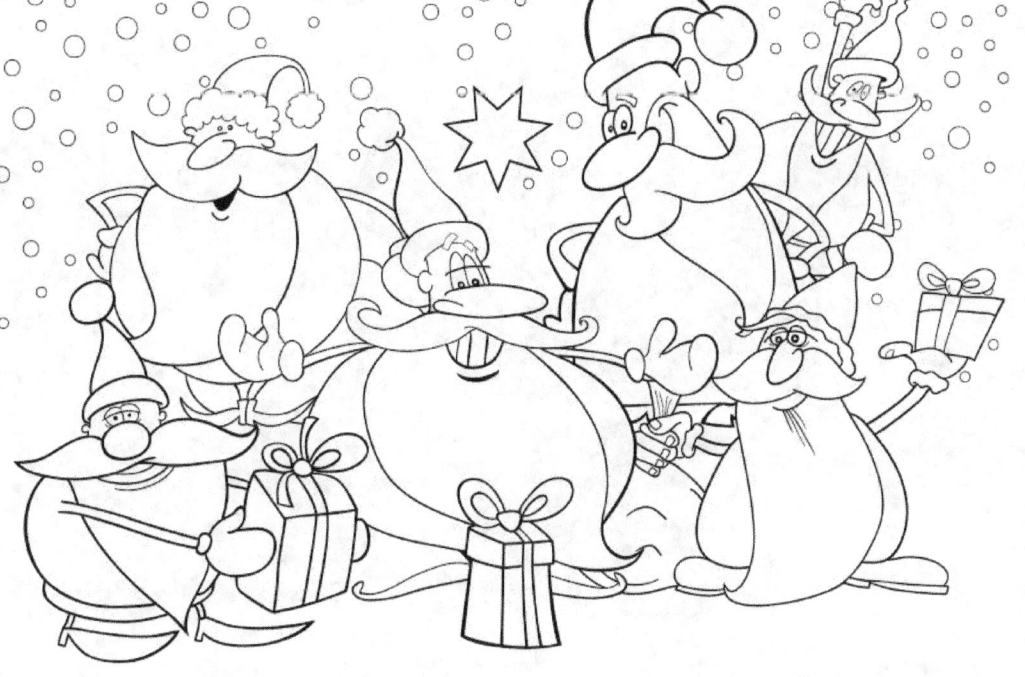

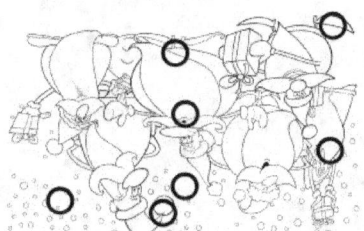

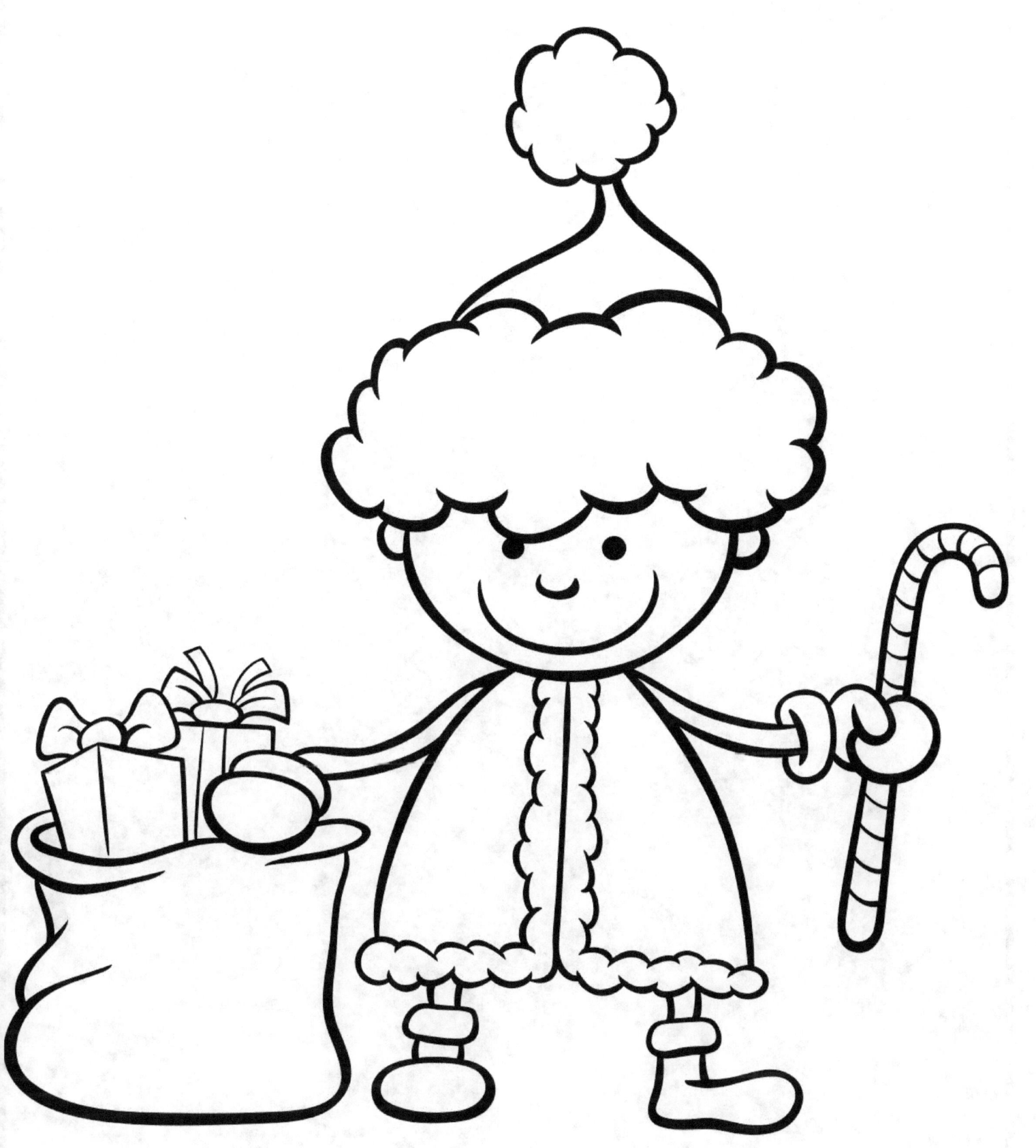

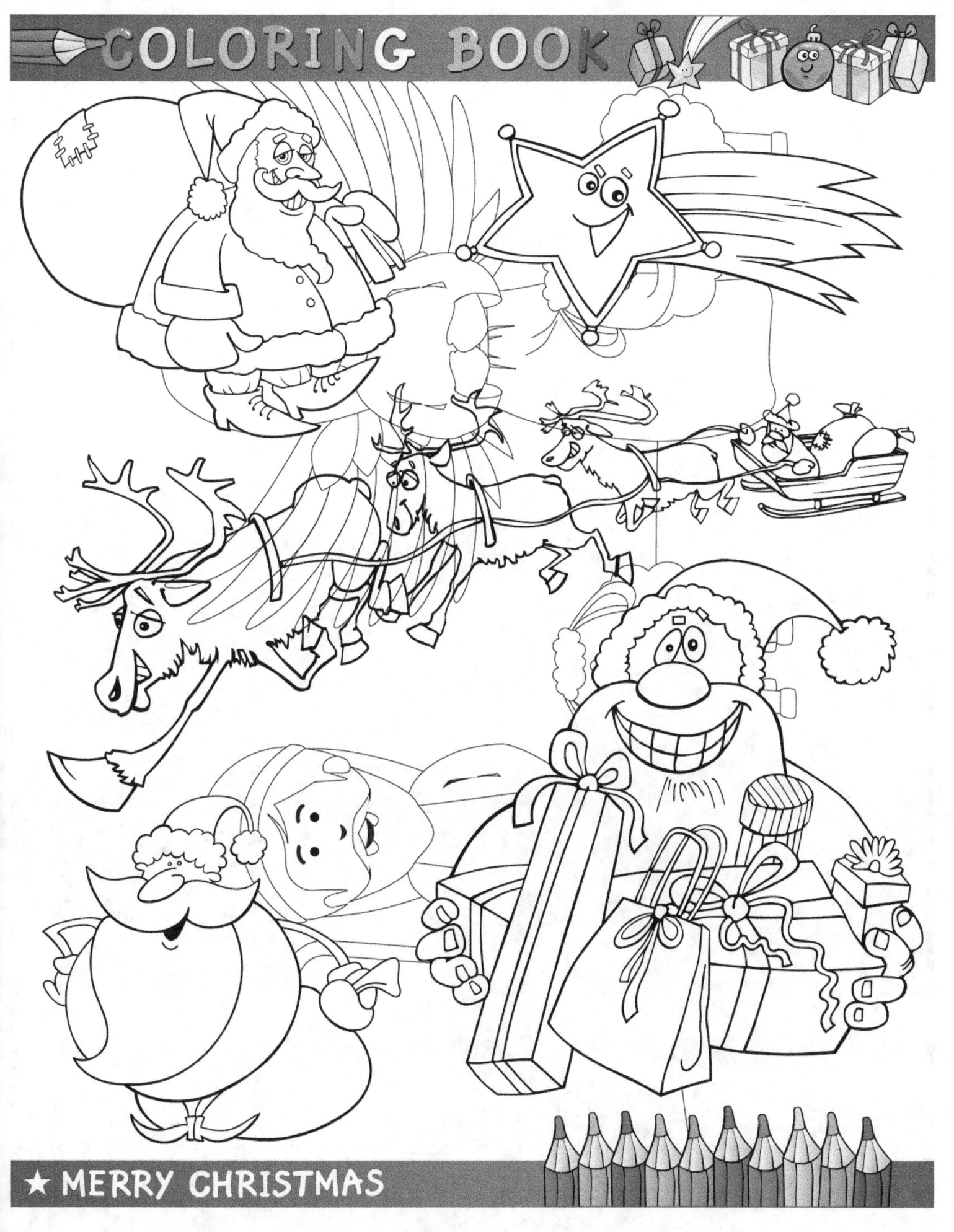

COLORING BOOK

★ MERRY CHRISTMAS

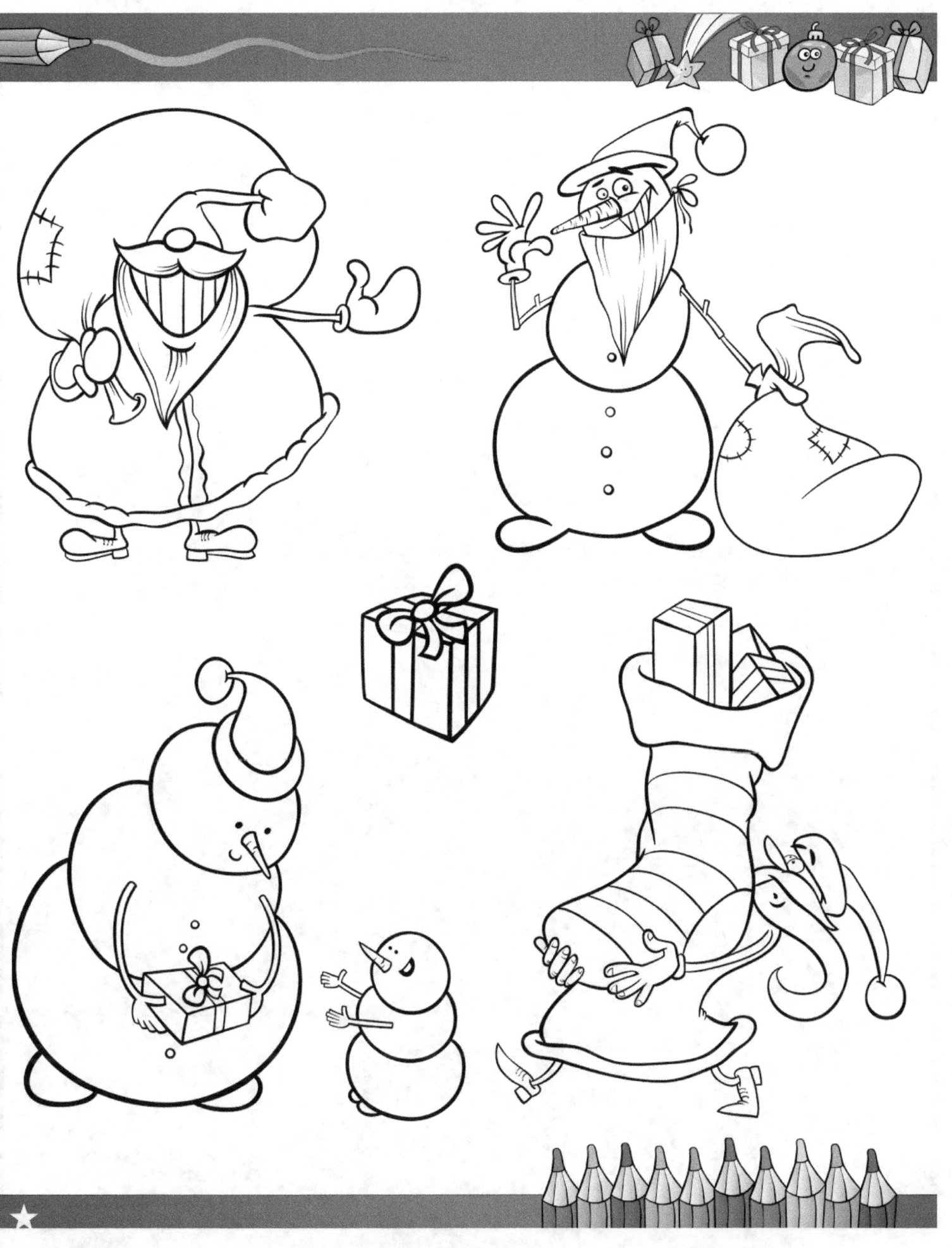

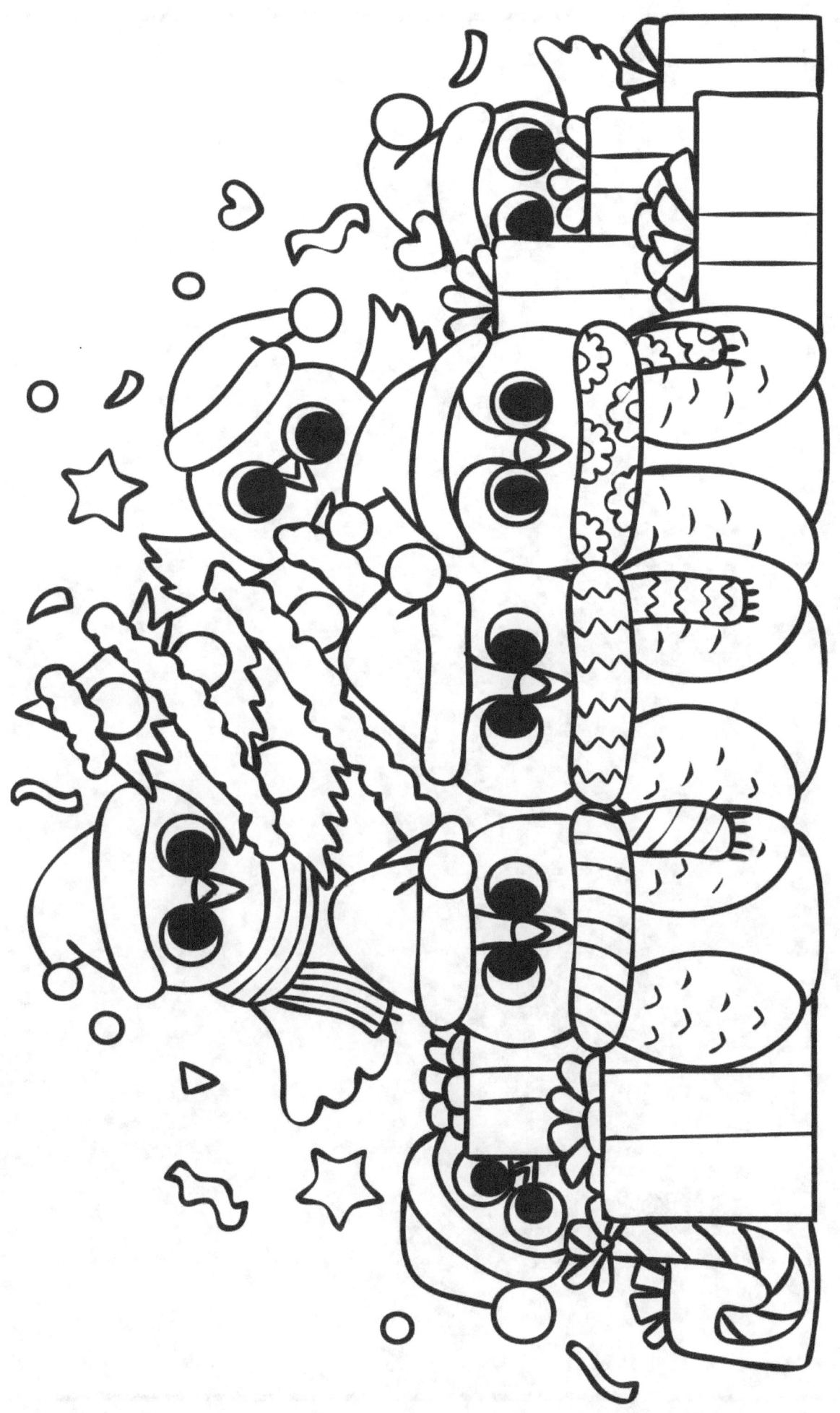

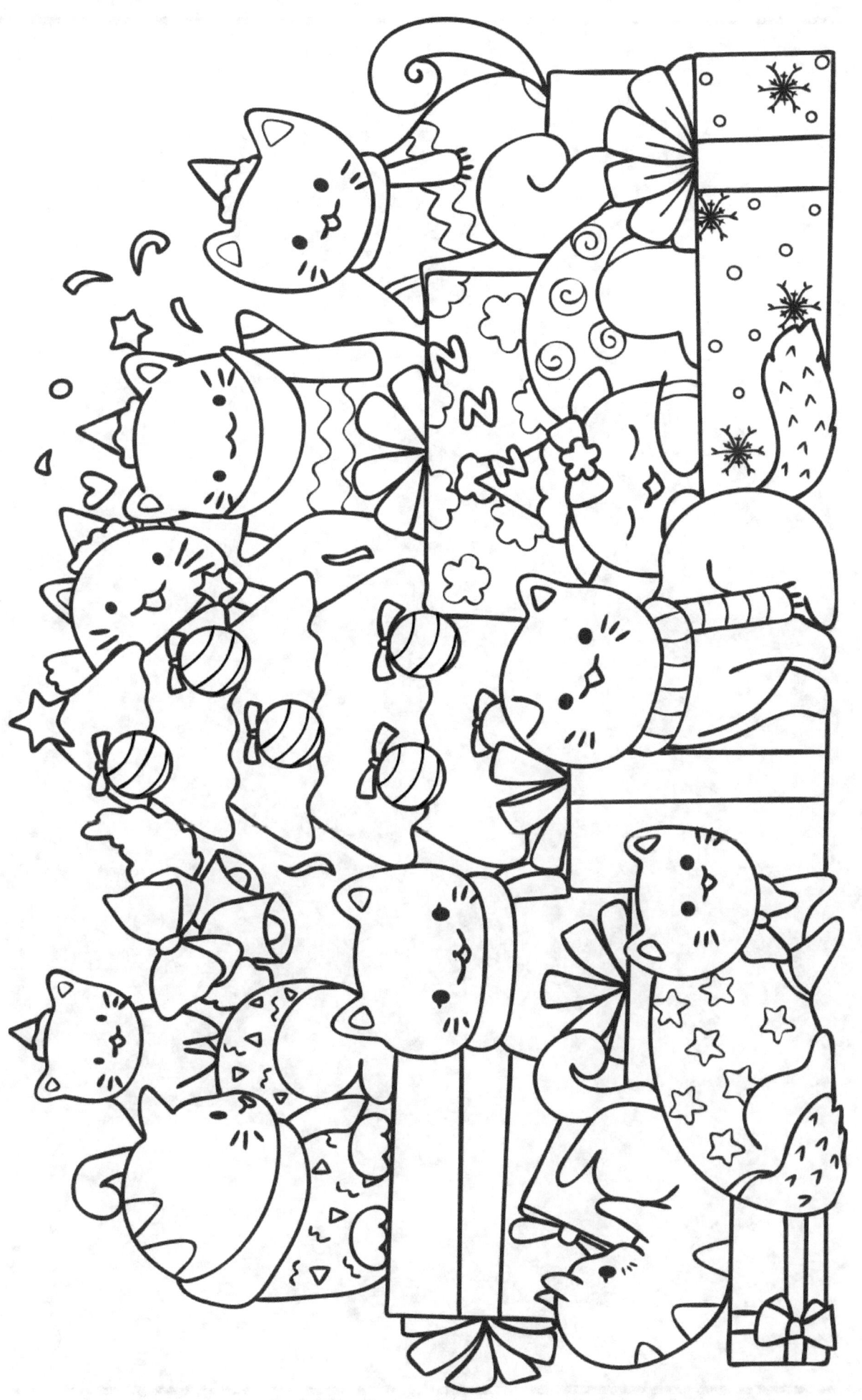

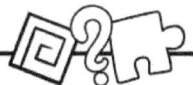

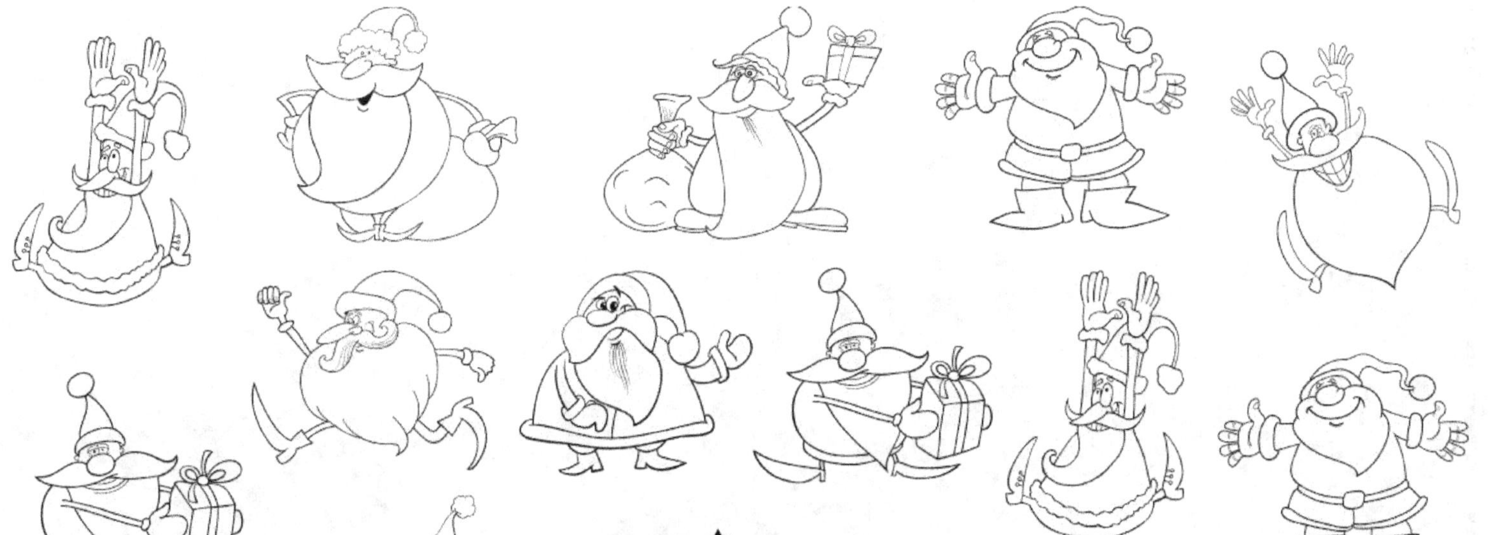

CHRISTMAS
FIND
ONE
OF A KIND

ANSWER

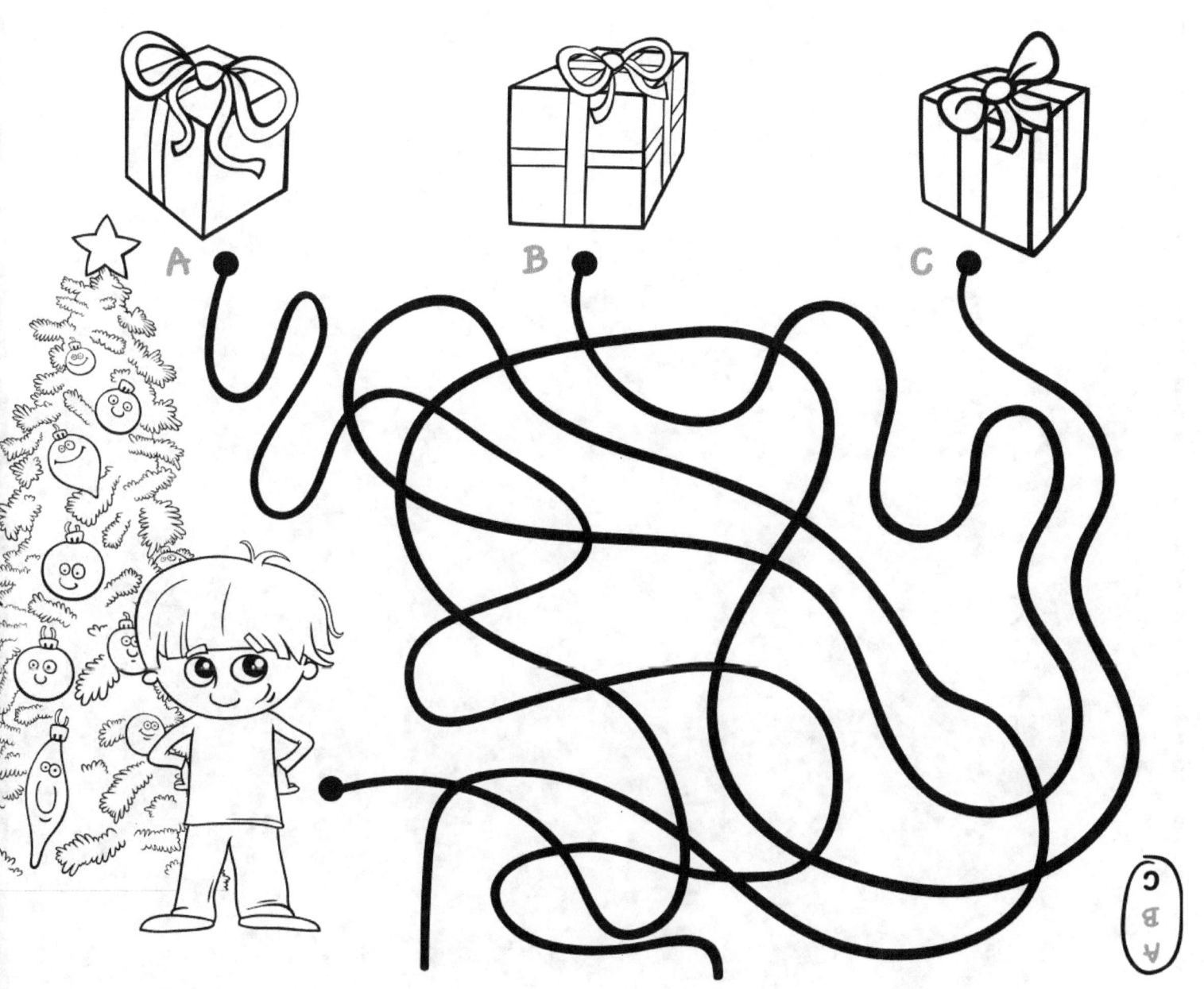

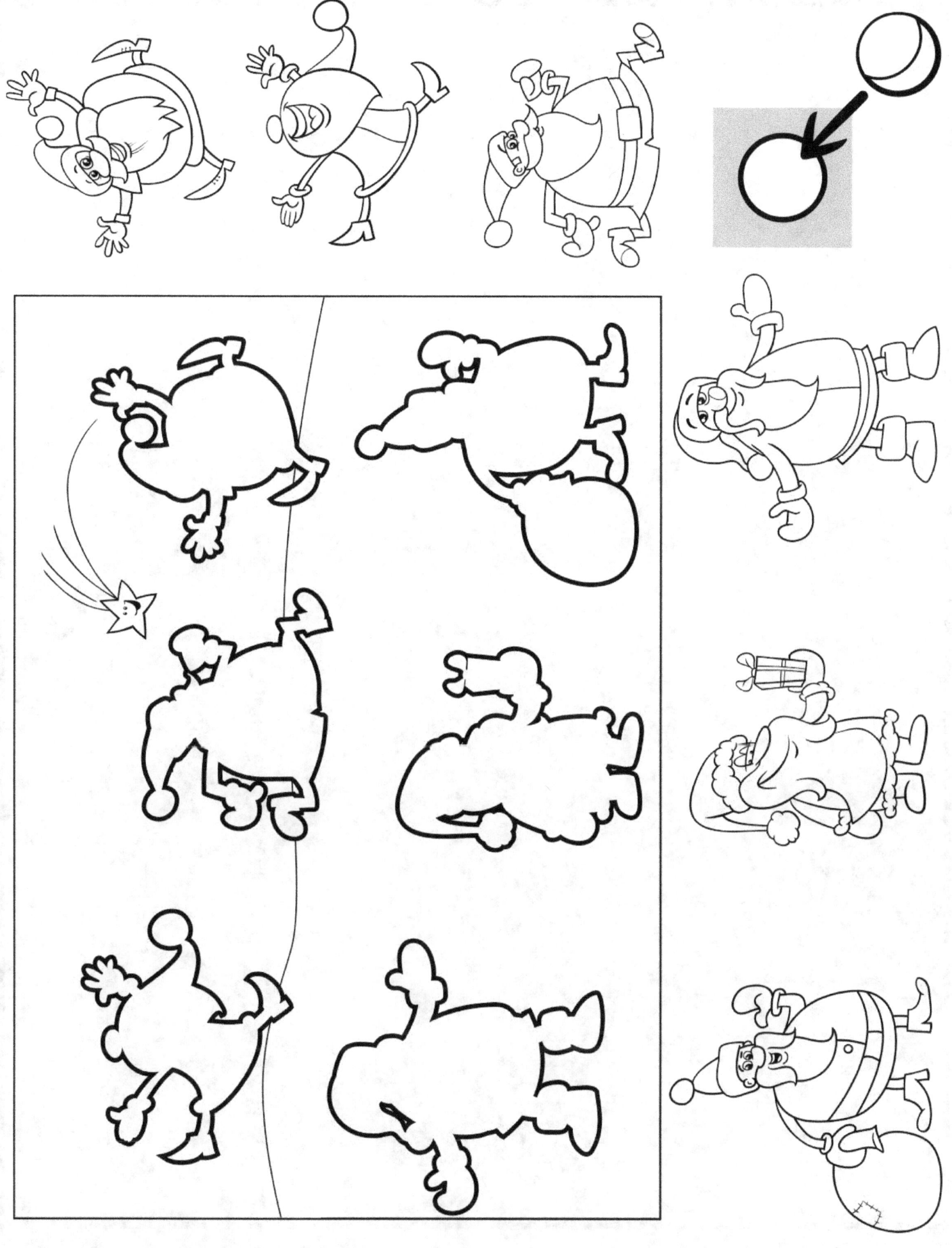

WHAT COMES NEXT?

1

2

3

4

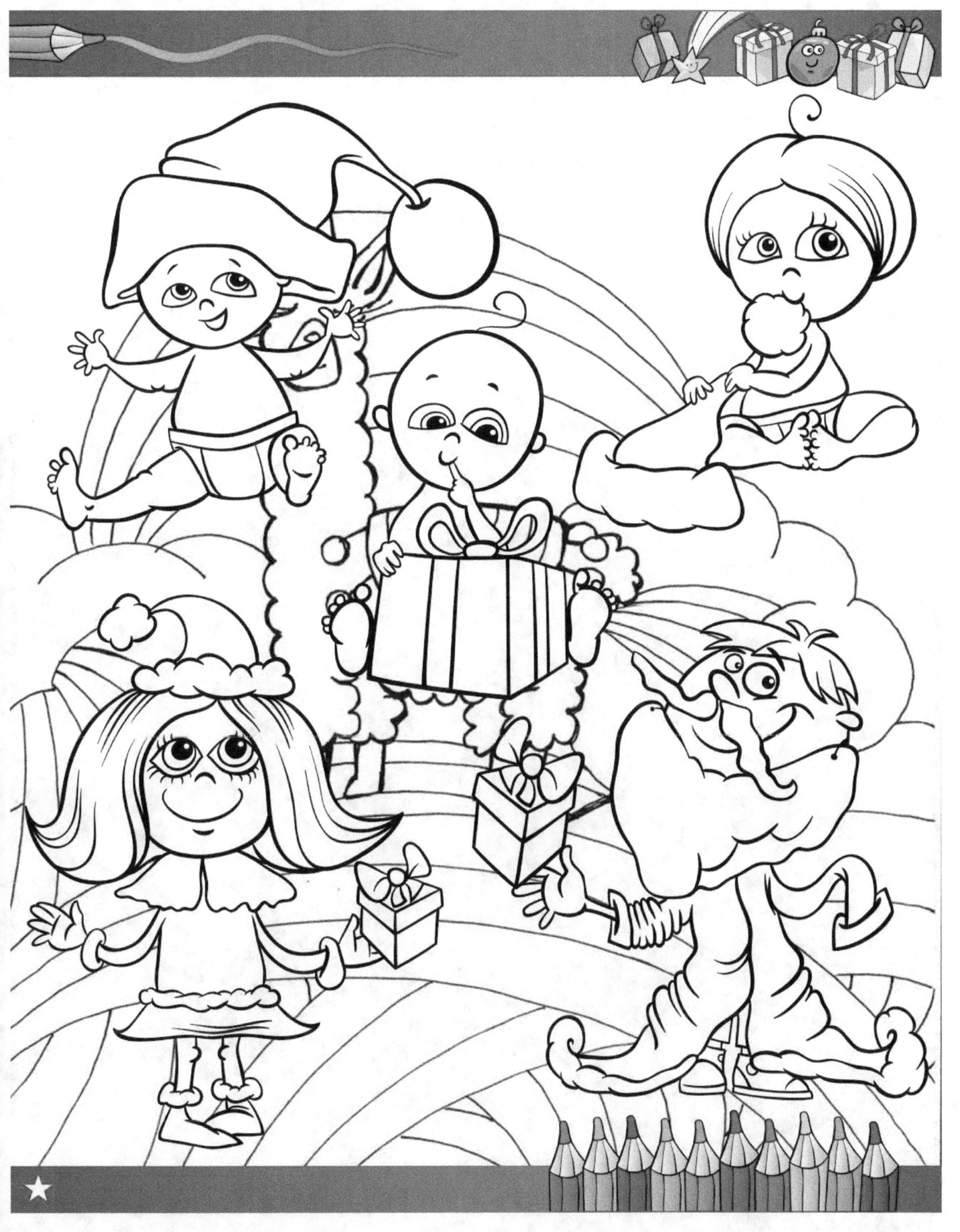

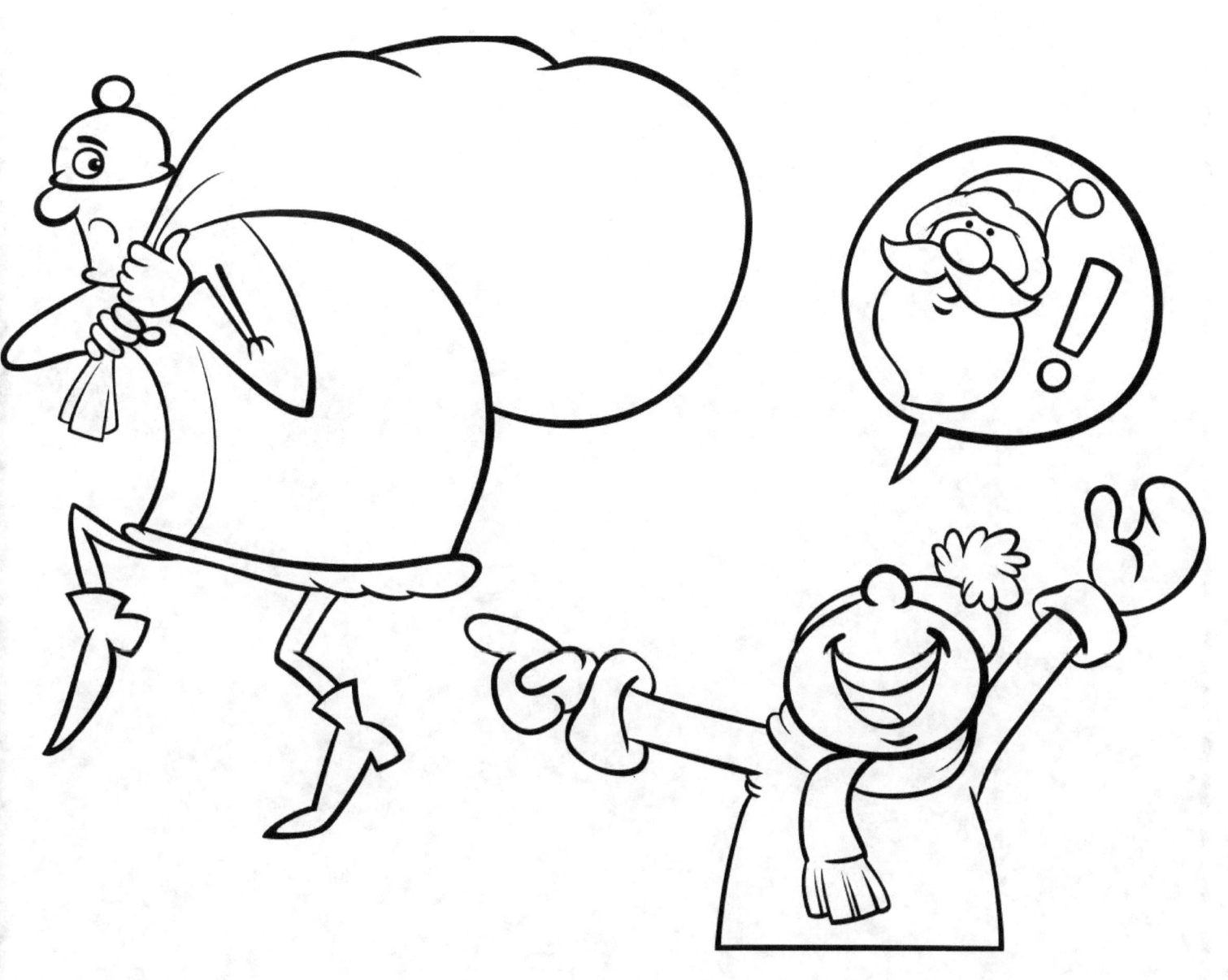

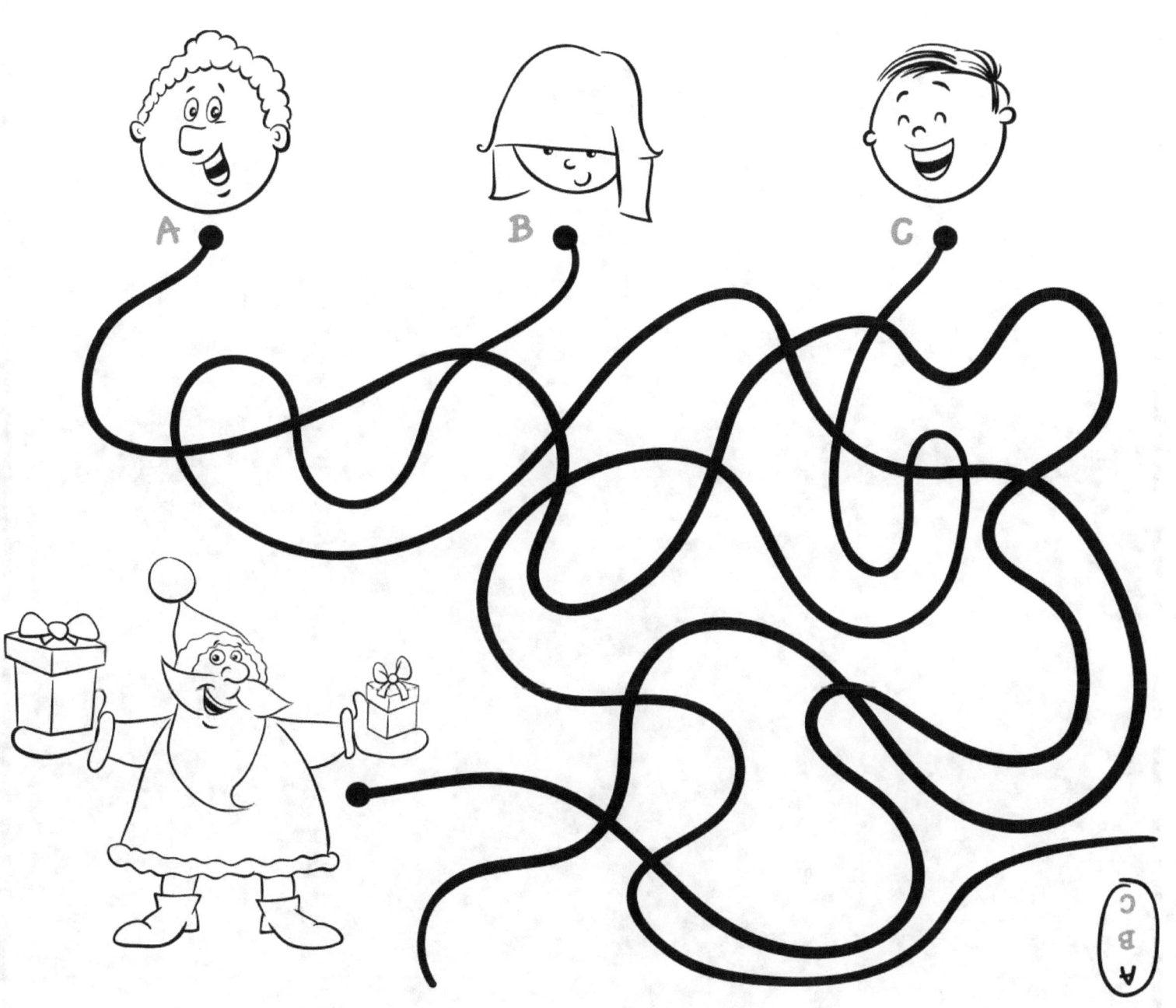

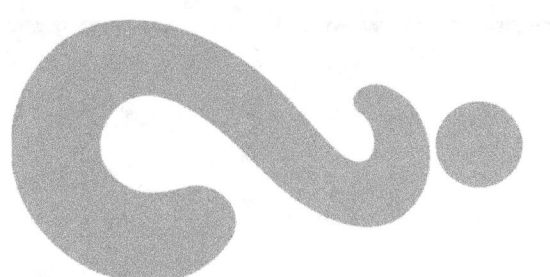

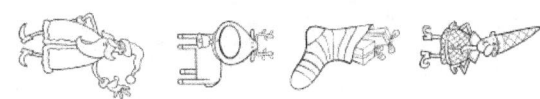

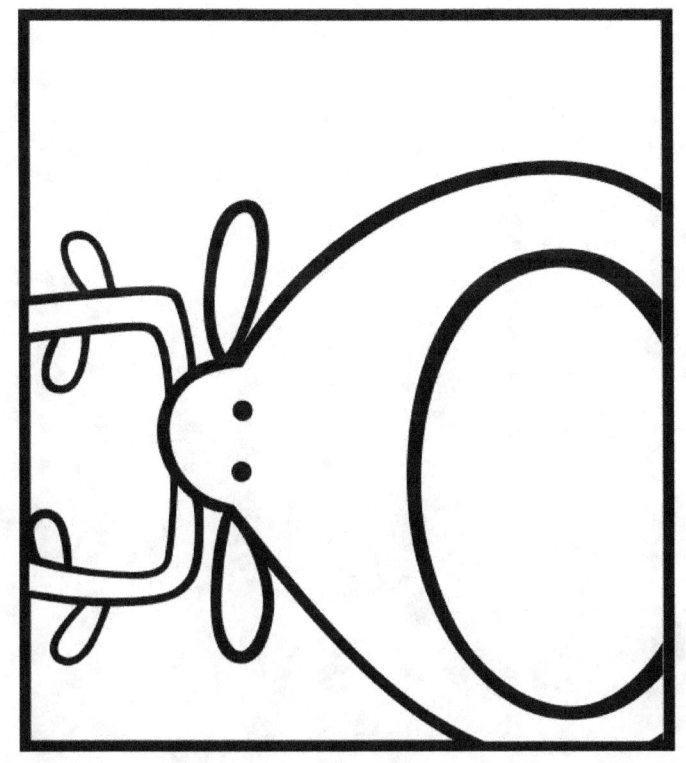

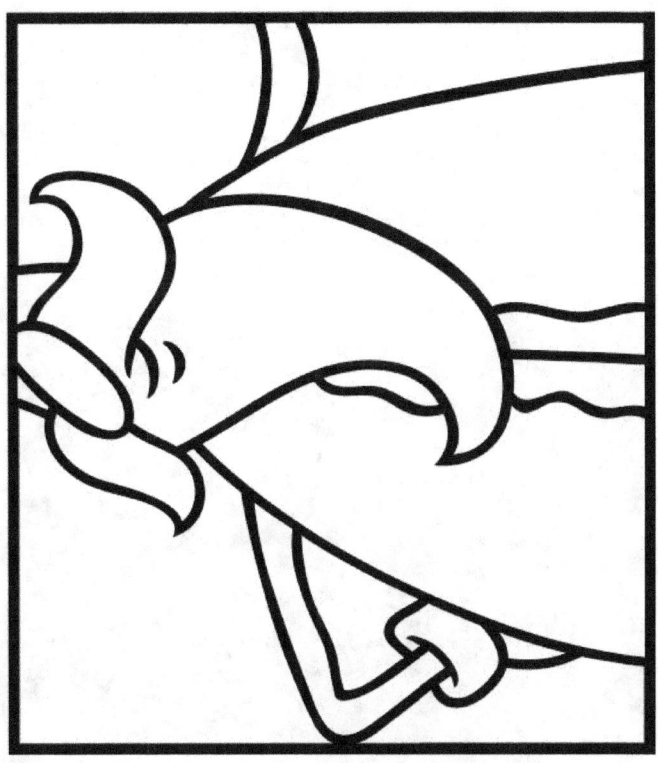

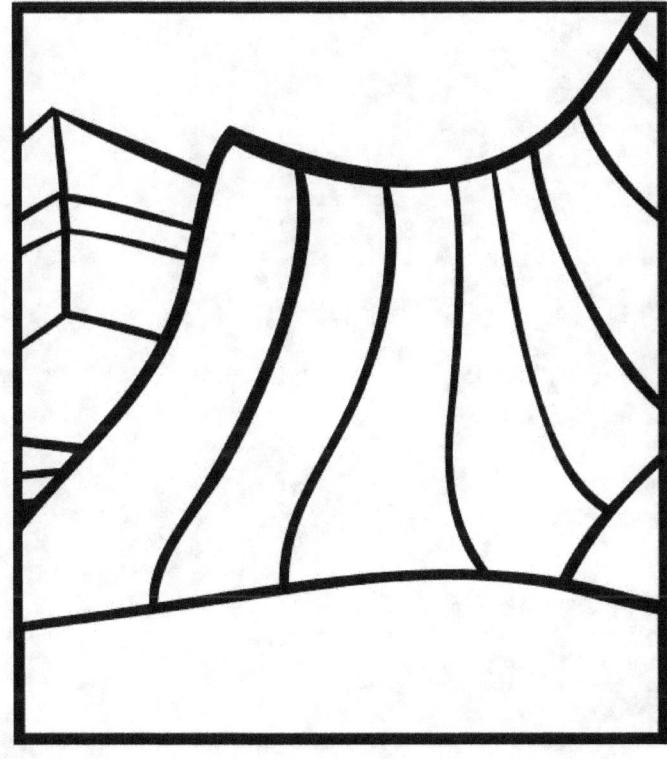

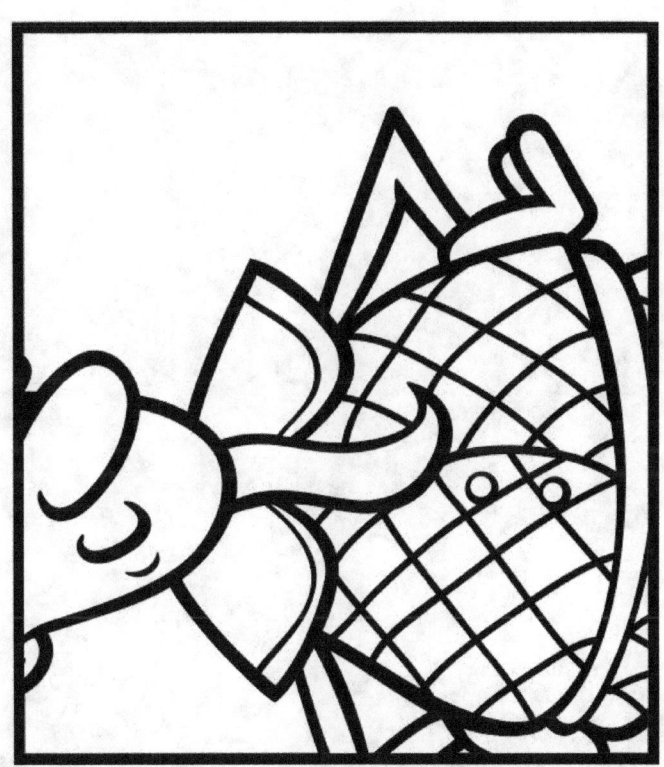

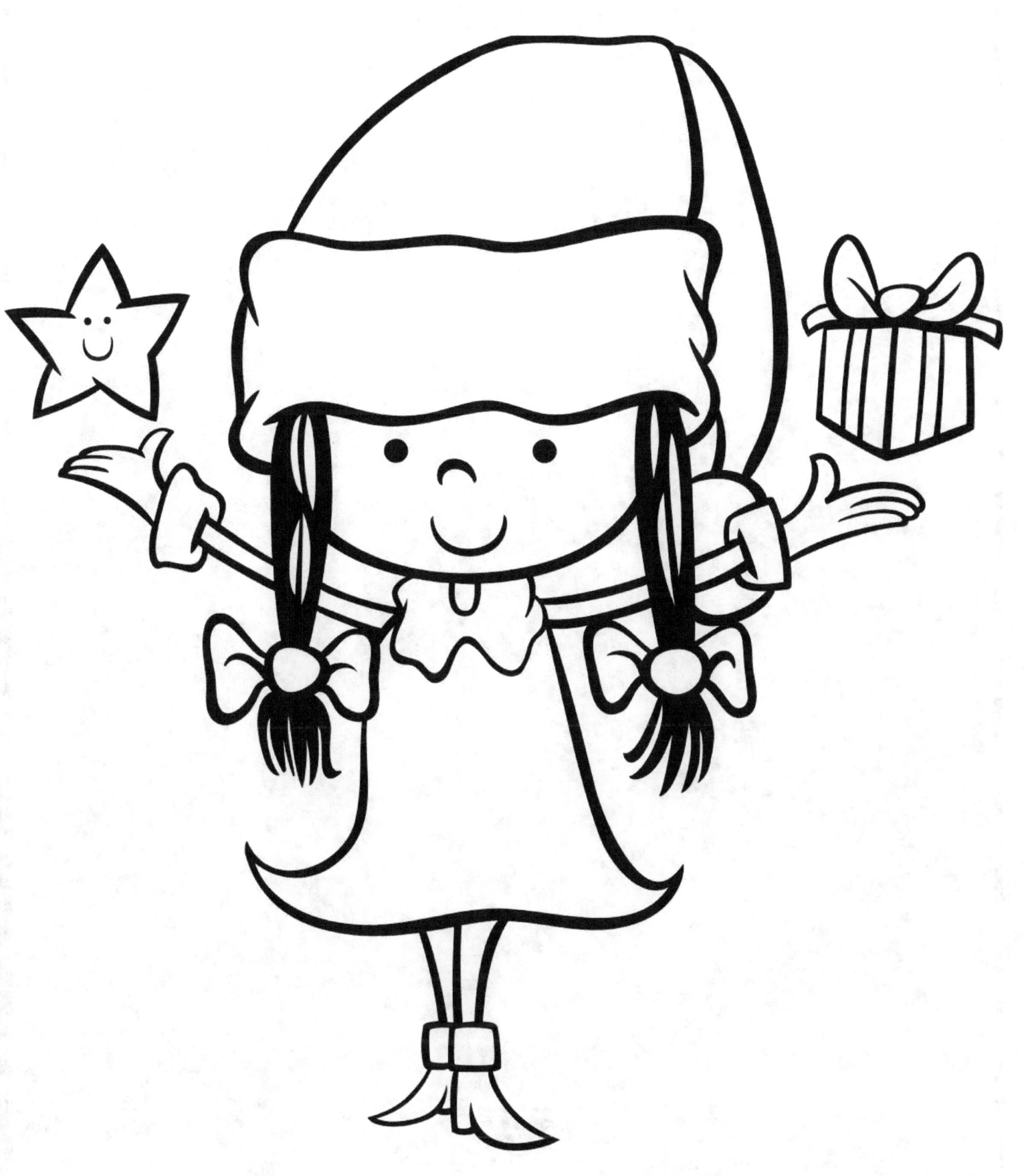

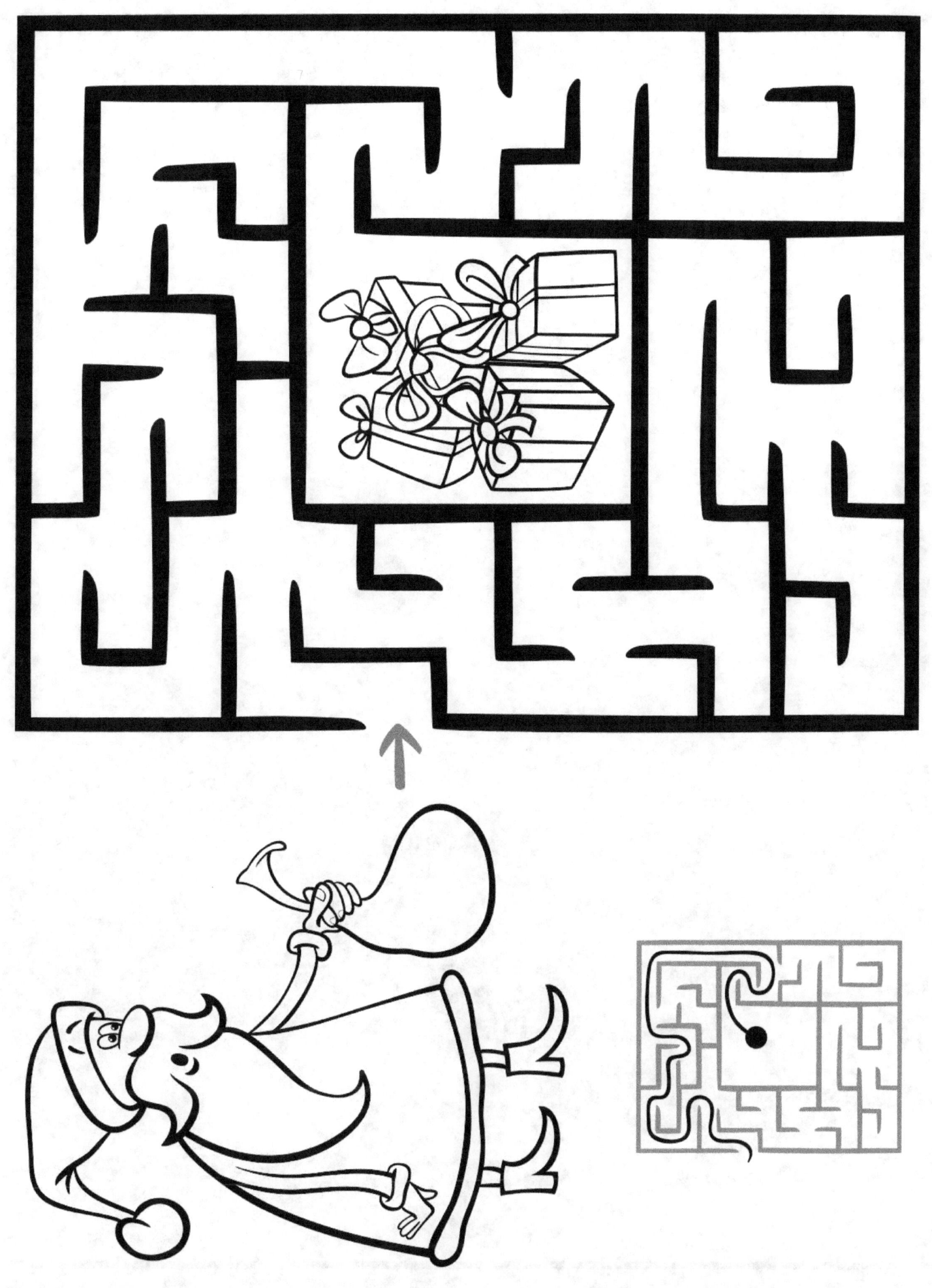

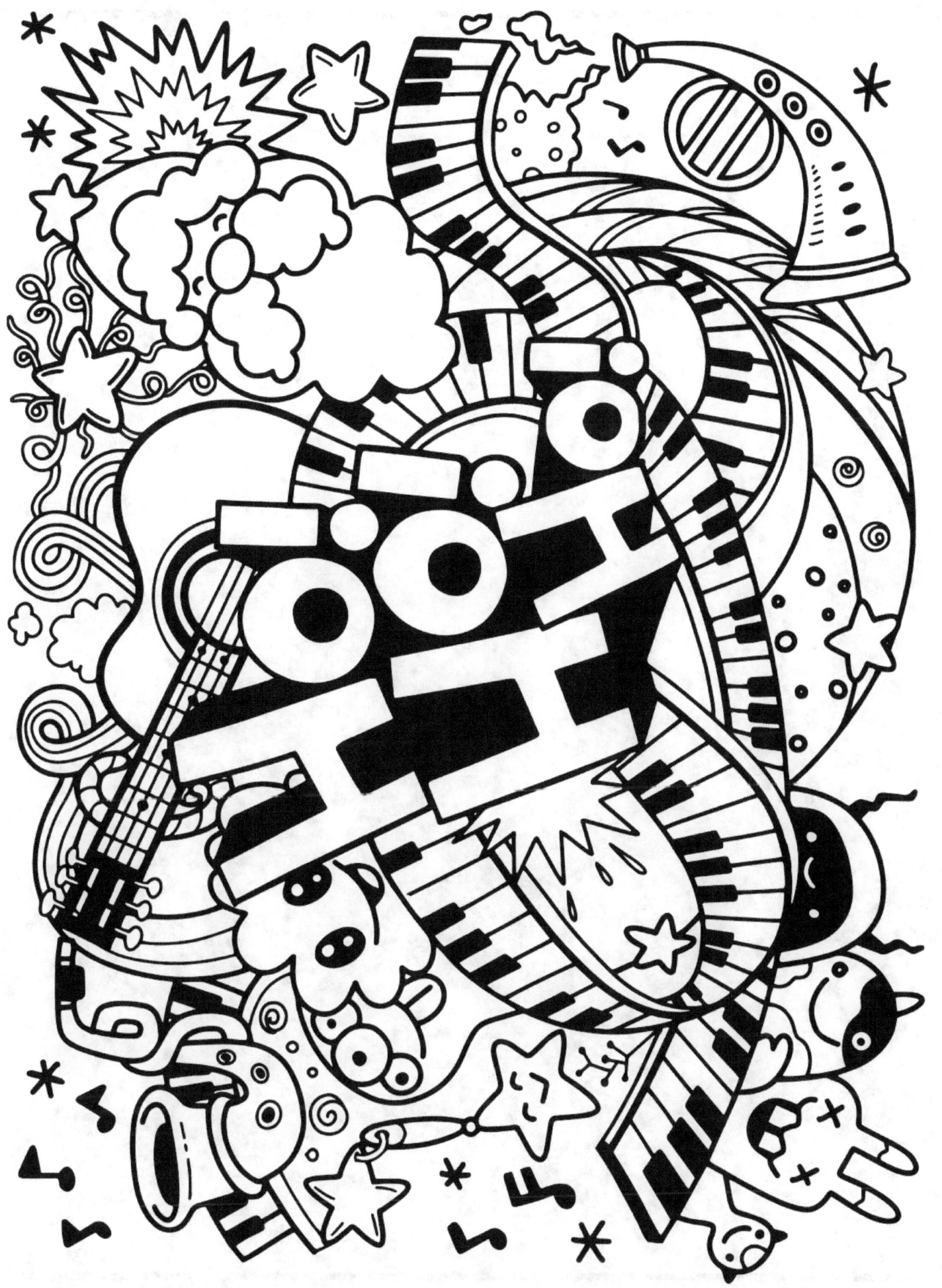

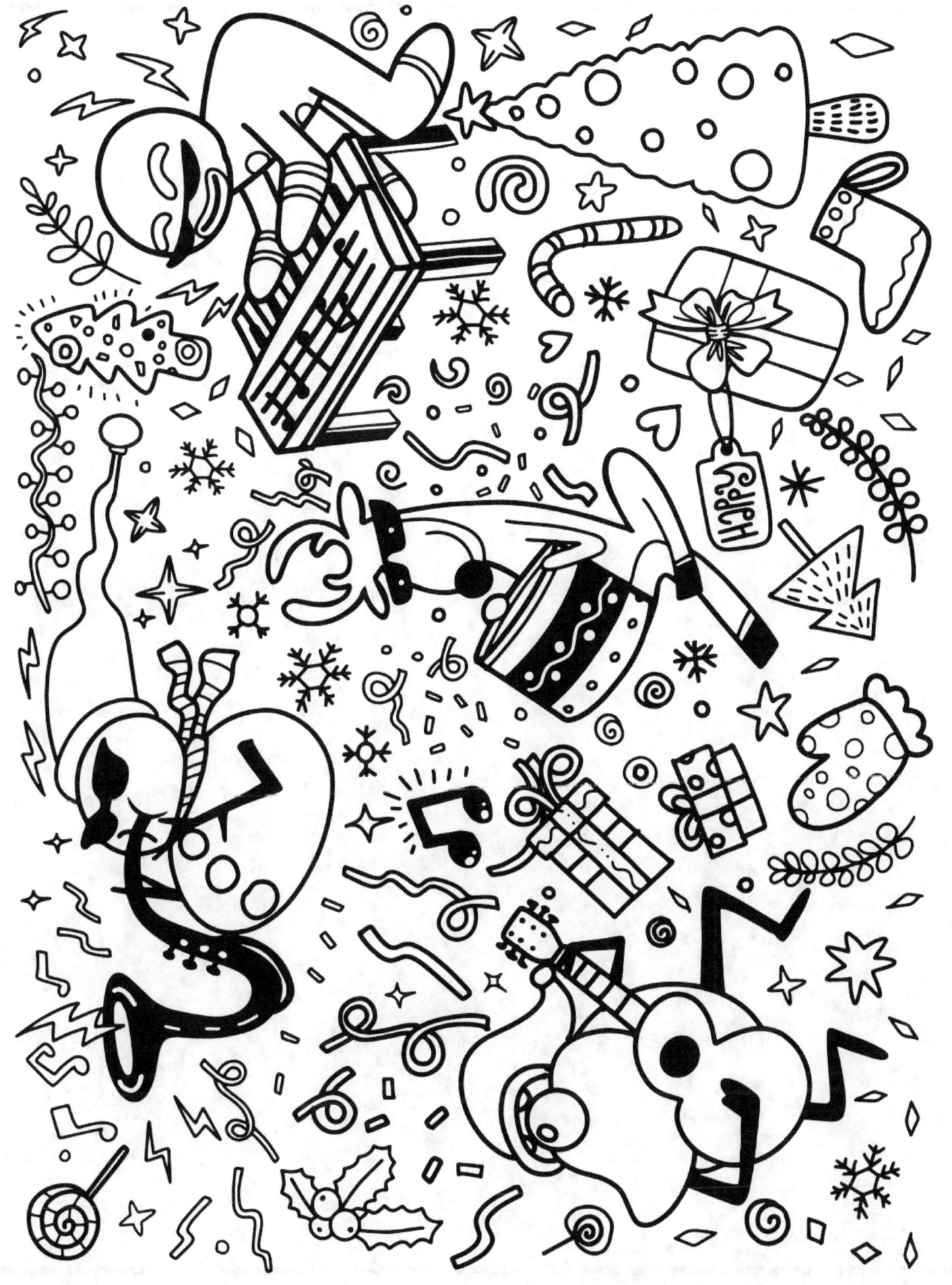

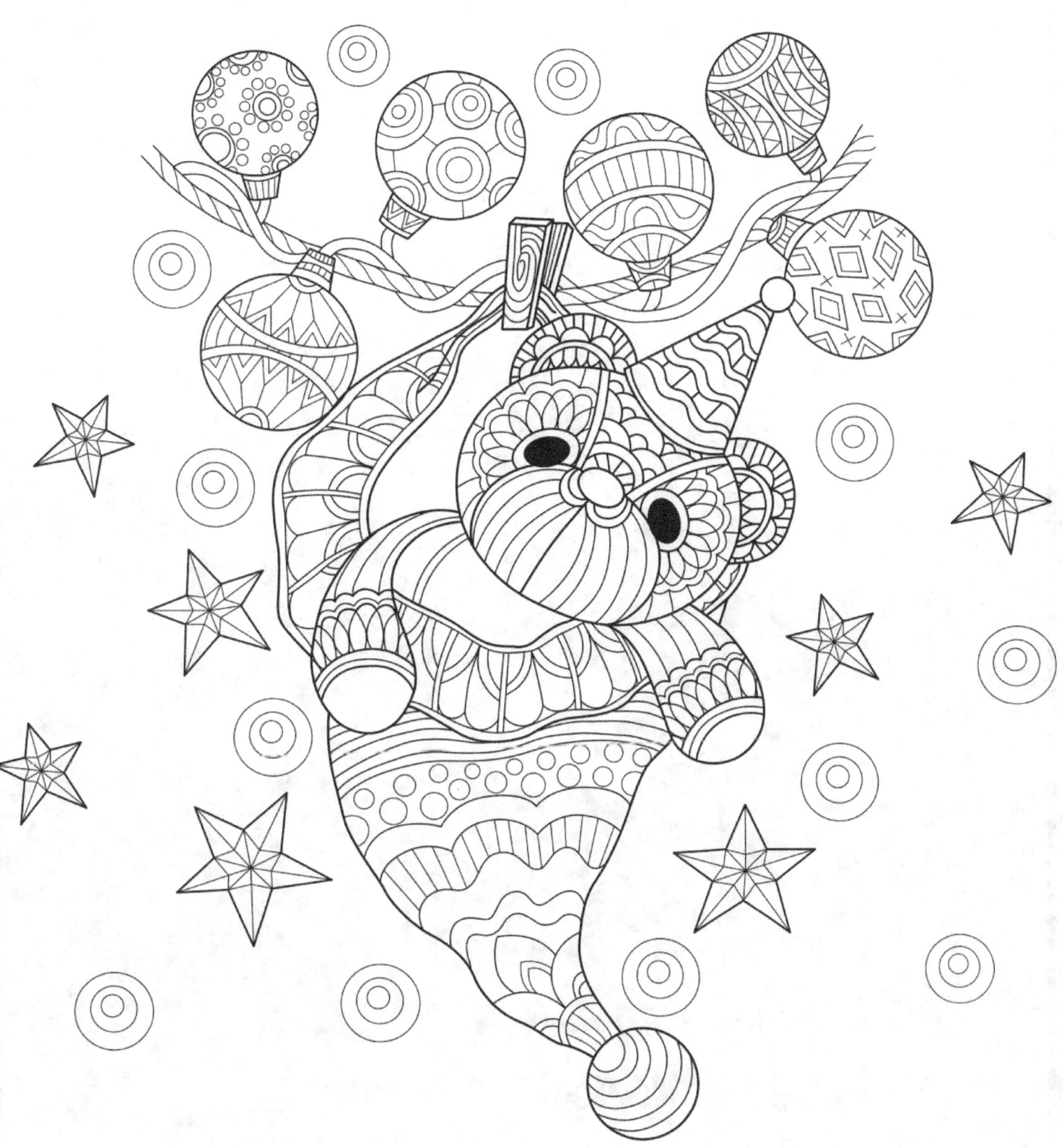

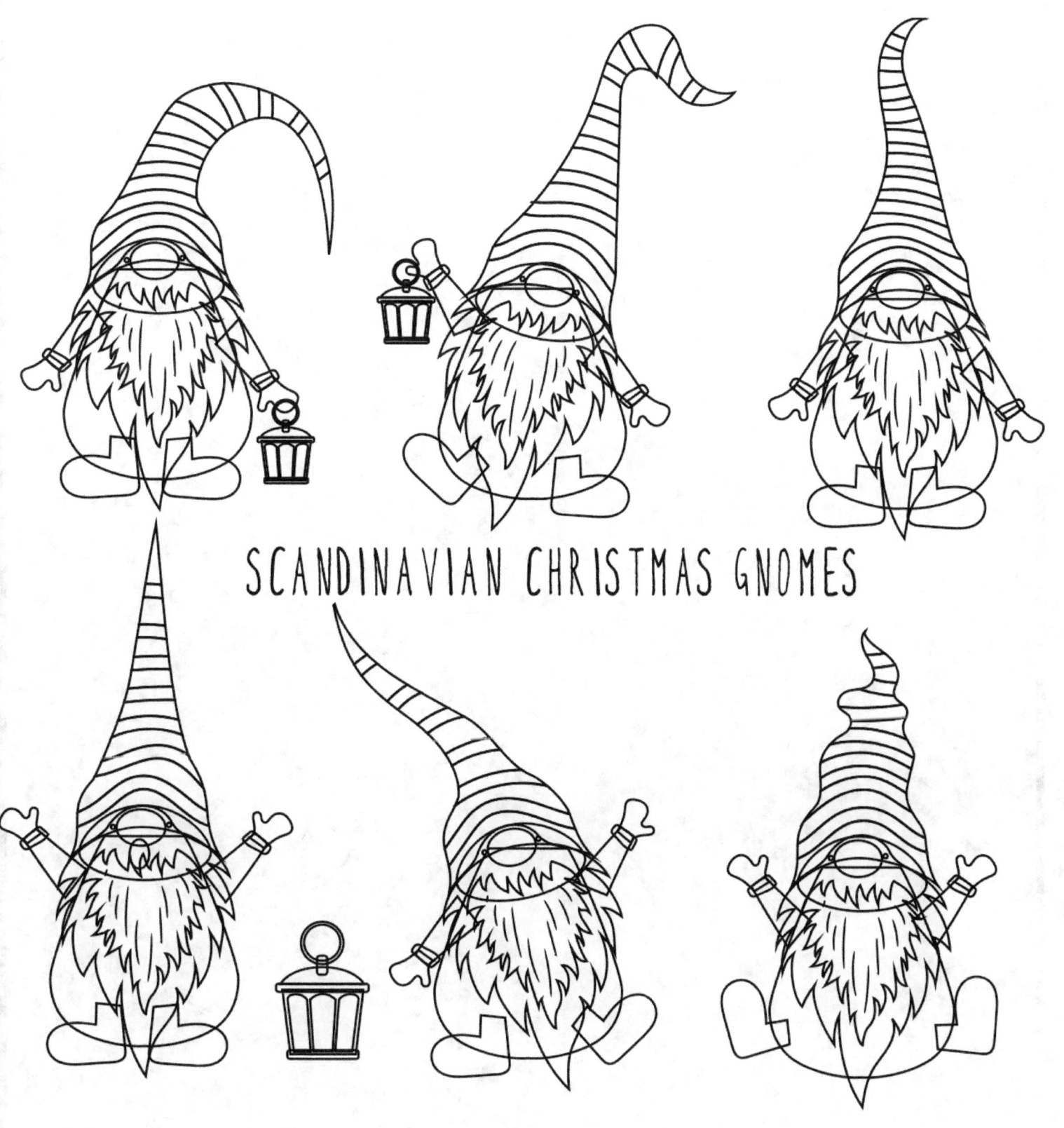

SCANDINAVIAN CHRISTMAS GNOMES